Too Close to the Sun

A Play Based on the Ancient Myth of Icarus

Janet Stutley
Illustrated by Mark Wilson

What Is a Myth?

Long ago, people made up stories to explain life and the world around them. These stories are called myths. This play is based on an ancient Greek myth.

The play has a chorus. A chorus is a group of people who speak together. Many ancient Greek plays had a chorus.

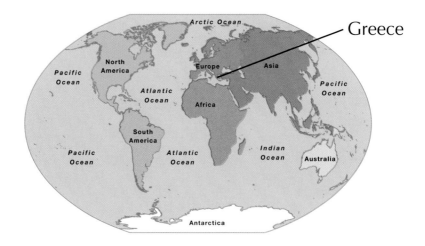

Characters

Daedalus *(DEH-duh-lus)*
A clever inventor

Icarus *(IH-kuh-rus)*
The son of Daedalus

Narrator   Chorus

Narrator: Long, long ago, there was a clever man named Daedalus. Daedalus and his son, Icarus, were prisoners on an island.

Icarus: Father, will we be here forever?

Daedalus: I hope not, son. But we've walked all around the island. I cannot see any way to escape.

Chorus: They walked for hours, all around. But no escape could be found.

Narrator: Daedalus and Icarus picked olives to eat. They collected honey from the wild bees. Every day, they looked at the sea and the sky.

Daedalus: Look at those seagulls! They are free—free as we can never be.

Icarus: Please, Father, don't give up hope!

Chorus: Don't give up! If you try, you can be free like birds in the sky!

Narrator: One day, Daedalus saw seagulls being lifted by the wind. Suddenly, he had an idea.

Daedalus: Icarus, I think I know how we can leave this island.

Icarus: How, Father?

Daedalus: We will learn to fly. It's the only way.

Chorus: Swift and free,
swift and free.
Birds fly high
above the sea.

9

Icarus: But we don't have
any wings, Father!

Daedalus: I've thought of something.
Help me gather up all these
seagull feathers.

Narrator: Icarus and Daedalus walked
all over the island, gathering feathers.
Then Daedalus collected wax
from the bee hives.

Chorus: Clever Daedalus,
you'll be free.
Icarus,
just wait and see!

11

Icarus: But why do we need feathers and wax, Father?

Daedalus: I'm going to make each of us a pair of wings. Then we can fly away from here.

Icarus: What a wonderful idea!

Chorus: You'll be free!
You'll be free!
Flying high
above the sea.

13

Narrator: Daedalus melted the wax and
used it to stick the feathers together.
He made two pairs of wings.
Icarus put on a pair
so he could practice flying.

Icarus: These wings are beautiful, Father.

Daedalus: Now we can fly away
from this island!

Chorus: Up and down,
up and down,
your wings will lift you
off the ground.

Narrator: Daedalus and Icarus walked to the top of a cliff by the sea.

Daedalus: Don't fly too close to the sun, Icarus! The wax will melt, and you will fall into the sea. And don't fly too close to the waves. The water will make the feathers wet, and you won't be able to fly.

Icarus: I'll do my best, Father.

Chorus: Listen, son, your father's right! Do as he says when you take flight.

17

Narrator: Then Daedalus and Icarus jumped from the cliff top and flew across the sea. The sun was very hot and bright.

Icarus: This is wonderful, Father! I can soar and swoop like a bird!

Daedalus: Remember what I told you. Stay away from the sun!

Chorus: Be careful
when you're in the sky.
It's dangerous
to fly too high!

Narrator: The wind lifted their wings and carried them far from the island.

Icarus: I want to go higher! Higher!

Daedalus: No, Icarus, come back! Come back! You are flying too close to the sun!

Chorus: Young Icarus,
beware, beware!
The wax will melt—
you must take care!

Narrator: But Icarus was too close
to the sun. The sun's heat
melted the wax on his wings.
The wings fell apart, and Icarus
tumbled into the sea.

Chorus: Down and down,
down and down.
Poor Icarus,
we fear, has drowned.

Narrator: Daedalus could do nothing
to save his son. He flew on
with tears in his eyes.

Daedalus: My son! My son!
If only you had listened to me!

Narrator: No one will ever forget
the story of Icarus.
The sea around the island
is now called the Icarian sea.
It is named after the boy who
flew too close to the sun.